My First Acrostic

Poets From Lancashire

Edited by Carole Hartwell

First published in Great Britain in 2010 by:

Young Writers

Young Writers
Remus House
Coltsfoot Drive
Peterborough
PE2 9JX
Telephone: 01733 890066
Website: www.youngwriters.co.uk

All Rights Reserved
© Copyright Contributors 2010
SB ISBN 978-1-84924-865-5

Foreword

The 'My First Acrostic' collection was developed by Young Writers specifically for Key Stage 1 children. The poetic form is simple, fun and gives the young poet a guideline to shape their ideas, yet at the same time leaves room for their imagination and creativity to begin to blossom.

Due to the young age of the entrants we have enjoyed rewarding their effort by including as many of the poems as possible. Our hope is that seeing their work in print will encourage the children to grow and develop their writing skills to become our poets of tomorrow.

Young Writers has been publishing children's poetry for over 19 years. Our aim is to nurture creativity in our children and young adults, to give them an interest in poetry and an outlet to express themselves. This latest collection will act as a milestone for the young poets and one that will be enjoyable to revisit again and again.

Contents

All Souls' CE Primary School
Oliver Chadwick (5)	1
Luke Thulborn (5)	2
Kacie Grayson (5)	3
Marisa Guild (5)	4
Nicky Horan (6)	5
Jake Meehan (5)	6
Zakk Garfield (5)	7
Grace Davis (5)	8
Asa Eden (5)	9
Lily Ryan (6)	10
Ben Taylor (5)	11
Olivia Corns (5)	12

Charlestown Community Primary School
Cobie Carew (6)	13
Sarah Touami (5)	14
Eboni Carter (6)	15
Keenan Brundrett (5)	16
Alice Song (5)	17
Kevin Gad (5)	18
Rebecca Pratt (6)	19
Johanka Saskova (5)	20
Jenny Zhao (6)	21
Amy McKinnon (6)	22
Bradley Leach (6)	23
Molly Wood (6)	24
DJ Birchall-Kenyon (6)	25
Charlotte Davey (7)	26
Kavakava Zervulana (7)	27
Jakob Williams (6)	28
Noor Afzal (6)	29
Kieran Chadwick (6)	30
Alex Keogh (7)	31
Megan Challoner (6)	32
Demi Leigh Parker (6)	33
Ethan Sleigh (6)	34
Vuyisile Khumalo (7)	35
Jessica Addy (6)	36
Chloe Cawley (6)	37

Cornholme JI&N School
Hollie Korobczyc (7)	38
Jack Curtis (7)	39
Mason Neil (6)	40
Elle Dyer (6)	41
Chloe Fish (6)	42
Mayah Brooks (6)	43
Oliver Link (6)	44
Alex Pendlebury (7)	45
Chloe Parker (6)	46
Bethany Lindley (6)	47
Tamar Stott (6)	48
Kyle Richardson (6)	49
Mirren Sunderland (6)	50
Mark Wheeler (6)	51

Deeplish CP School
Hina Ihsan (7)	52
Zohaib Azam (6)	53
Maryam Mahmood (5)	54
Marium Ashfaq (5)	55
Hafsa Khan (5)	56
Sadiqah Fatima Bibi (6)	57
Hafsa Ul-Haq (7)	58
Raihaan Ufran (6)	59
Zain Malik (6)	60
Sulaimaan Muhammad Ali (7)	61

Gisburn Road CP School
Sam Waddington & Cameron Pearce (5)	62
Kai Frankland (5)	63
Alisha Amer (5)	64
Anthony Collinge (6)	65
Tilly Falshaw (6)	66
David Atkinson (6)	67
Charley Berry (6)	68
Abid Zia & Kyle Rowan (6)	69
Abigail Noon (5)	70

Lathom Park CE Primary School
Beth Fairclough (6)	71
Niamh Jefferson (5)	72
James Sharrock (7)	73

Ella Hutchinson (5) 74
Mia Aldred (6) 75
Daniel Fogarty (4) 76
Lily Sharrock (4) 77

Littleborough CP School
James Kerr (6) 78
Megan France (6) 79
Nathan Browne (6) 80
Liam Simpson (6) 81
Archie Catlin (7) 82
Harry Ramsbottom (6) 83
Saffron Poskitt (6) 84
Freya Hollis (6) 85
Millie Harris (6) 86
Emily Dorrington (6) 87
Harvey Barker (7) 88
Matthew Williamson (6) 89
Adam Baker
& Jacob Cockcroft (6) 90
Grace Shepherd 91
Christopher Howarth 92

Manley Park Primary School
Aadil Sarwar (6) 93
Finn Moorhouse (6) 94
Hannah Iqbal (6) 95
Imaan Talha (6) 96
Amanda MacKenzie (6) 97
Aqeel Ahmed (6) 98
Zaina Dar (6) 99
Mandeep Landa (7) 100
Isabella Rowles-Bennett (6) 101
Arooj Shakoor (6) 102
Max Barrett (6) 103
Abir Ahmed (6) 104
Kiana Queeley (6) 105
Raj Abbas (7) 106
Cinderella Group (6) 107
Snow White Group (6) 108
Beanstalk Group (6) 109
Gingerbread Man Group (6) 110
Goldilocks Group (6) 111

Markland Hill CP School
Chhaya Patel (6) 112
Madelaine Ramsden (6) 113
Nabilah Thagia (6) 114

Oliver Leach (6) 115
Isobel Alice Jones (6) 116
Grace Sohor (6) 117
Callum Thomas Oldfield (6) 118
Ellis Richardson (6) 119
Benjamin Hunt (5) 120
Sam Davenport (5) 121
Lucas Russell (5) 122
Hannah Lay (5) 123
Luke Anderson (5) 124
Ellie Rafferty (6) 125
Summer Kay (5) 126
Jasmine Lily Patel (6) 127
Sasha Palmer (6) 128
Kian Mistry (5) 129
Helena Lathwell-Watts (5) 130
Anuj Mishra (5) 131
James Bewley (7) 132

St Joseph's RC Junior School, Leigh
Cara Knowles (6) 133
Ellie Taylor McDermott (6) 134
Shannon Roberts (6) 135
Rebecca Clegg (6) 136
James Clegg (6) 137
Ben McDermott (6) 138
Amelia Tyrer (6) 139
Hollie Hunter (7) 140
Cerys Knowles (6) 141
Fiona Wilkinson (6) 142
Ellie Shepherd (6) 143
Jack Bamford, Joshua Hedley,
Louis Jackson Newn (6)
& Aiden Dungey (7) 144
Rebecca Wakefield (7) 145

St Oswald's CE Primary School, Blackburn
Julia Woodworth (5) 146
Jack Crossley (5) 147
Jacob Crawford (5) 148
James Flynn (5) 149
Samantha Savage (5) 150
Ellessa Williamson (5) 151
Mariyah Ahmed (5) 152
Hafsah Zubair (5) 153
Brooklyn Spiers (5) 154

Addison Cosgrove (5) 155
Mia Dickinson (5) 156
Lucas Kennedy (5) 157
Joshua McDonald (5) 158
Joseph Campbell (5) 159
Domenico Nelson (6) 160
Cameron Carruthers (6) 161
Joshua Parrington (6) 162
Faye Filbin (6) 163
Corey Walsh (6) 164
Scott Duffy (6) 165
Fatima Lodge (6) 166
Joe Banks (6) 167
Lewis Heyn (6) 168
Brandon Parkinson (6) 169
Louise Cullen (6) 170
Abbie Bausor (6) 171
Bailey Madden (6) 172

Sacred Heart Catholic Primary School
Alex Burrows (6) 173
Ebony Pennington (7) 174
Nathan James Daly (6) 175
Sam Birch (6) 176
Davis Lythgoe (6) 177
Oliver Whittle (7) 178
Matthew Best (6) 179
Anna Zwolinska (6) 180
Lennon Pennington (6) 181
Adam Pilkington (6) 182
Joshua Cain (6) 183
Aidan Dickinson (6) 184
Richard Nelson (6) 185

Turton & Edgworth Primary School
Phoebe Banks (6) 186
Erin Louise Gardiner (5) 187
Isaac Earnshaw (5) 188
Rebecca Sheldon (5) 189
Daisy Grace Mather (5) 190
Joshua Aubrey (6) 191
Libby Faye Roberts (5) 192
James White (6) 193
Aneurin Walsh (5) 194
James Joseph Fox (5) 195

Watersheddings Primary School
Libby Bradbury (7) 196
Hana Karim (6) 197
Joseph Sargent (6) 198
Nicole Sweeney (6) 199
Sarah-Jane McDonald (6) 200
Lara Bardsley (6) 201
Paiden Ball (7) 202

The Poems

Crash

C ars are fantastic
R ed is good
A nd has stripes
S hiny and new
H oot! Hoot!

Oliver Chadwick (5)
All Souls' CE Primary School

Football

F ootball is good
O ff the line
O n the line
T evez
B oot
A rsenal are good
L iverpool are the best
L ine again.

Luke Thulborn (5)
All Souls' CE Primary School

My First Acrostic - Poets From Lancashire

Kacie Grayson

K ind and caring
A mazing Kacie
C olouring is good
I ce cream is nice
E gg is my favourite food

G orgeous I am
R eally good I am
A rt I love
Y oung and fun
S ongs are good
O n time I am
N ever naughty.

Kacie Grayson (5)
All Souls' CE Primary School

Hanna Montana

H ilarious Hanna
A mazing Hanna
N o one is better than Hanna
N ice friends
A lot of fans she has

M oney she's got to buy stuff
O n stage she is the best
N ice hair
T o be like me
A better star
N o one is better
A mazing fans.

Marisa Guild (5)
All Souls' CE Primary School

My First Acrostic - Poets From Lancashire

Football

F ive good players
O n the line
O ver the line
T evez is the best in the world
B oots are muddy
A mazing Liverpool
L iverpool are the best in the whole world
L ampard, you missed.

Nicky Horan (6)
All Souls' CE Primary School

Skeleton

S kull
K id skeleton
E lbow
L eg
'**E** llo
T onight
O riginal
N aughty.

Jake Meehan (5)
All Souls' CE Primary School

… My First Acrostic - Poets From Lancashire

School

S chool is good and exciting
C hildren kick into the net
H appy
O li hops in the playground
O ranges in school
L earn in school.

Zakk Garfield (5)
All Souls' CE Primary School

School

S chool is good
C hildren play nicely
H arris isn't happy
O liver is really nice
O livia is beautiful
L ily is good.

Grace Davis (5)
All Souls' CE Primary School

My First Acrostic - Poets From Lancashire

School

S it down on the carpet
C oats in the playground
H elp people at school
O n the carpet
O n the playground
L ook for people.

Asa Eden (5)
All Souls' CE Primary School

School

S inging with Miss Willis
C ounting
H orses are my favourite
O h, amazing Lily
O n the carpet we sit
L ots of friends.

Lily Ryan (6)
All Souls' CE Primary School

Toys

T oys are to play with
O n my Wii
Y ou are going down
S orry for knocking.

Ben Taylor (5)
All Souls' CE Primary School

Football

F erdinand is the best
O n the line
O n the pitch
T en players
B oots on
A ston Villa are the best
L iverpool are the best
L ine again.

Olivia Corns (5)
All Souls' CE Primary School

My First Acrostic - Poets From Lancashire

Space

S un was as bright as a space rocket
P lanets playing zoom in space
A liens from number Zork watch
C obie dancing then
E veryone was dancing!

Cobie Carew (6)
Charlestown Community Primary School

Space

S hooting stars are twinkling in the sky

P urple cats are eating on the moon

A liens won't stop dancing on the moon

C akes are left in space

E llis won't stop eating on the moon.

Sarah Touami (5)
Charlestown Community Primary School

Space

S tars sparkle in space
P lanets float around space
A liens dance
C raters are dark
E very alien has tentacles.

Eboni Carter (6)
Charlestown Community Primary School

Space

S hining stars up in space
P ainting aliens, painting Pluto
A liens dancing on the moon
C ameron can't stop catching comets
E llis won't stop eating on Earth!

Keenan Brundrett (5)
Charlestown Community Primary School

Space

S omeone was going to the moon
P ast the stars, the planets
A nd the moon was big
C at was on the moon too
E yes look up into the sky.

Alice Song (5)
Charlestown Community Primary School

Space

S hooting stars
P lanets going around the sun
A liens and astronauts playing together
C ats in space calling the comets
E lephants crunching the moon!

Kevin Gad (5)
Charlestown Community Primary School

My First Acrostic - Poets From Lancashire

Space

S hooting stars sparkle in space
P lanet Pluto saying 'Please'
A liens on an angry planet
C amouflaged in space
E nergetic alien running everywhere.

Rebecca Pratt (6)
Charlestown Community Primary School

Space

S prinkle stars all round space
P retty planets
A liens are funny but not in Africa
C omets are colourful and
E arth is with the moon.

Johanka Saskova (5)
Charlestown Community Primary School

My First Acrostic - Poets From Lancashire

Dinosaurs

D inotastic.
I nteresting bones.
N aughty creatures.
O ld fossils in the rocks.
S harp teeth to bite.
A ngry eyes.
U nusual feet.
R oar all the time.

Jenny Zhao (6)
Charlestown Community Primary School

Dinosaurs

D inosaur
I nterpreting
N oisy
O ld
S cary
A mazingly
U nusual
R oar.

Amy McKinnon (6)
Charlestown Community Primary School

My First Acrostic - Poets From Lancashire

Dinosaurs

D inosaurs are scary.
I nteresting faces.
N asty dinosaurs.
O ld dinosaurs.
S cary eyes.
A big tooth.
U nusual lips.
R ough body.

Bradley Leach (6)
Charlestown Community Primary School

Dinosaurs

D inosaur
I nteresting
N oisy, noisy
O ld, old
S cary, scary
A mazing, amazing
U nusual, unusual
R oar, roar.

Molly Wood (6)
Charlestown Community Primary School

My First Acrostic - Poets From Lancashire

Dinosaurs

D inosaurs are interesting
I nteresting bones
N asty dinosaurs
O ld dinosaurs
S cary face
A ngry teeth
U gly tails
R ough body.

DJ Birchall-Kenyon (6)
Charlestown Community Primary School

Dinosaurs

D ragons
I nteresting
N oisy
O ld
S limy
A ngry dinosaurs
U nusual
R oar.

Charlotte Davey (7)
Charlestown Community Primary School

Dinosaur

D angerous
I nteresting
N oisy
O ld
S cary
A mazing
U nusual
R oar.

Kavakava Zervulana (7)
Charlestown Community Primary School

Dinosaurs

D aft dinosaurs.
I nteresting names.
N ecks are long.
O ld dinosaurs.
S tegosaurus have sharp teeth.
A ngry dinosaurs.
U nusual dinosaurs.
R eally dangerous.

Jakob Williams (6)
Charlestown Community Primary School

My First Acrostic - Poets From Lancashire

Dinosaurs

D angerous dinosaurs.
I nteresting fossils to look at.
N aughty animals.
O ld bones to look at.
S trong tails to smash things.
A ngry T-rex chased triceratops.
U nderground you find fossils.
R oar very loudly.

Noor Afzal (6)
Charlestown Community Primary School

Dinosaurs

D angerous tyrannosaurus rex chased velociraptor
I nteresting dinosaur fossil
N ecks are long and big
O ld dinosaurs are gone by now
S trong tyrannosaurus rex are the world's strongest dinosaurs
A nd they have long necks
U nusually long necks are very heavy and hard tails
R oar very loudly.

Kieran Chadwick (6)
Charlestown Community Primary School

My First Acrostic - Poets From Lancashire

Dinosaurs

D inotastic
I nteresting fossils
N asty face
O ld dinosaurs
S piky things
A nd dinosaurs are big
U nderground fossils
R uns around
S cary eyes.

Alex Keogh (7)
Charlestown Community Primary School

Dinosaurs

D inotastic
I nteresting
N ot alive
O ld
S cary
A ngry
U nhappy
R oar.

Megan Challoner (6)
Charlestown Community Primary School

My First Acrostic - Poets From Lancashire

Dinosaurs

D inosaurs are nasty.
I nteresting dinosaurs.
N oisy dinosaurs.
O range are some dinosaurs.
S cary are some dinosaurs.
A ngry are some dinosaurs.
U gly are some dinosaurs.
R ough are some dinosaurs.

Demi Leigh Parker (6)
Charlestown Community Primary School

Dinosaurs

D inotastic
I nteresting creatures
N oisy animals
O ld fossils are under the ground for thousands of years
S tegosaurus are vegetarian
A ngry
U nder the ground are fossils
R oars very loudly.

Ethan Sleigh (6)
Charlestown Community Primary School

My First Acrostic - Poets From Lancashire

Dinosaurs

D inosaurs are scary.
I ncredible size and big teeth.
N asty eyes and big teeth.
O lder dinosaurs were bigger than a house.
S teamy dinosaurs that could fly.
A nkylosaurus was a big animal but not as big as a T-rex.
U nusual faces.
R ushing to eat other dinosaurs.
S cary and horrible teeth.

Vuyisile Khumalo (7)
Charlestown Community Primary School

Dinosaurs

D ino.
I nteresting dinosaur.
N oisy T-rex.
O ld dinosaur.
S tegosaurus can be noisy.
A ngry, nasty T-rex.
U gly T-rex.
R oaring, annoying dinosaur.

Jessica Addy (6)
Charlestown Community Primary School

My First Acrostic - Poets From Lancashire

Dinosaurs

D inosaurs are nasty.
I nteresting dinosaurs.
N asty dinosaurs.
O ld dinosaurs.
S cary dinosaurs.
A dinosaur is surprising.
U gly dinosaurs.
R ough dinosaurs.

Chloe Cawley (6)
Charlestown Community Primary School

Hedgehog

H ibernate

E at insects

D ark nights

G rass gets wet

E verywhere

H edgehogs have to keep warm

O ctober is cold

G rass has frost.

Hollie Korobczyc (7)
Cornholme JI&N School

My First Acrostic - Poets From Lancashire

Conkers

C runch of the leaves
O range
N ature
K eys freeze
E very leaf falls to the floor
R ed leaves
S olid wood.

Jack Curtis (7)
Cornholme JI&N School

Colder

C older
O ctober
L eaves
D ecember
E xcitement
R ain falls.

Mason Neil (6)
Cornholme JI&N School

Acorn

A utumn
C onkers
O utside
R ainy days
N uts.

Elle Dyer (6)
Cornholme JI&N School

Autumn

A corn
U mbrella
T ree
U ntidy leaves
M ushrooms
N uts.

Chloe Fish (6)
Cornholme JI&N School

Hedgehog

- **H** ungry
- **E** ats insects
- **D** elightful
- **G** athers food
- **E** xtremely funny
- **H** appy
- **O** ctober
- **G** reat.

Mayah Brooks (6)
Cornholme JI&N School

Hedgehog

H ibernate
E xquisite spikes
D angerous
G round homes
E xcellent defenders
H urtful if they prick you
O ut at night
G reat sight.

Oliver Link (6)
Cornholme JI&N School

Hibernate

H appy
I cy ground
B reathing slows
E xcellent conkers
R ich leaves
N ature
A corns gathered
T own frosty
E ating nuts.

Alex Pendlebury (7)
Cornholme JI&N School

Autumn

A pples
U nusual
T rees
U mbrellas needed
M igrate
N ights get darker.

Chloe Parker (6)
Cornholme JI&N School

Hedgehog

H ides for the winter
E ats insects
D ark earlier
G olden skin
E xcellent at hiding
H ollow brain
O ld spikes
G reat at finding food.

Bethany Lindley (6)
Cornholme JI&N School

Hedgehog

H appy
E xcellent
D rink
G athers food
E at
H ibernates
O nly comes out at night
G rows spikes.

Tamar Stott (6)
Cornholme JI&N School

My First Acrostic - Poets From Lancashire

Owl

O range
W ings
L ikes to fly.

Kyle Richardson (6)
Cornholme JI&N School

Guy Fawkes

G uard
U nconscious
Y eoman

F ire
A ge 50
W ounded
K ing
E xecuted
S word.

Mirren Sunderland (6)
Cornholme JI&N School

Hedgehog

H ibernate
E at
D rinks
G ets lots of food
E xcellent spikes
H ides
O range
G reat.

Mark Wheeler (6)
Cornholme JI&N School

Manchester

M y favourite day is going to Manchester.
A nyone can go to Manchester.
N ew toys are in Manchester.
C ome with us to Manchester.
H appy times when we go to Manchester.
E veryone comes from far away.
S ee cars on Eid when we go to Manchester.
T oday I am going to Manchester.
E very day we get ice cream from Manchester.
R ains a lot in Manchester.

Hina Ihsan (7)
Deeplish CP School

My First Acrostic - Poets From Lancashire

Zohaib

Z ooming Zohaib
O strich
H andsome
A mazing boy
I maginative boy
B est boy.

Zohaib Azam (6)
Deeplish CP School

Maryam

M agical
A mazing
R ed
Y oghurt
A mazing
M ysterious.

Maryam Mahmood (5)
Deeplish CP School

My First Acrostic - Poets From Lancashire

Marium

M agic
A fter
R un
I ce cream
U sually incredible
M agical.

Marium Ashfaq (5)
Deeplish CP School

Hafsa

H appy
A nt
F ancy
S ad
A mazing.

Hafsa Khan (5)
Deeplish CP School

Holidays

H appy days
O n the aeroplane I went to Pakistan
L ovely time
I went to Liverpool and I went on the ships
D ad took me to the funfair
A nd I got a present
Y es it is springtime
S chool is closed.

Sadiqah Fatima Bibi (6)
Deeplish CP School

Sister

S ee me go to Asda and find a doll.
I give ice cream to my friends.
S ummer is very hot and a little bit cold.
T he ice cream van gives lots of ice cream.
E veryone plays with my sister.
R uns and comes down which my sister likes.

Hafsa Ul-Haq (7)
Deeplish CP School

My First Acrostic - Poets From Lancashire

The Beach

T omorrow I am going to Blackpool beach
H ope the weather is going to be perfect
E xcellent day to go to the beach

B lue sea waves and the sky is blue
E xcellent day to go on rides
A lways my mum buys me ice cream
C ream is my favourite food
H ope I have a fun day at the beach.

Raihaan Ufran (6)
Deeplish CP School

In The Shop

In the sweet shop
Nice things to buy and taste

The shop is big
Has lots of sweets
Everyone goes to the sweet shop

Some penny sweets
Hula Hoops and crisps
Orange juice to drink
Polos are my favourite sweet.

Zain Malik (6)
Deeplish CP School

My First Acrostic - Poets From Lancashire

Cricket

C ome and play cricket.
R un and catch the ball.
I am playing cricket.
' C ome home now,' says Mum.
K now that I am hungry
E ggs are cooking in the kitchen
T eeth are falling out of my mouth.

Sulaimaan Muhammad Ali (7)
Deeplish CP School

My Senses - Hearing

H ooting owls
E lephants trumpeting
A eroplanes zooming
R oaring lions
I n the jungle
N oisy screaming children
G urgling water.

Sam Waddington & Cameron Pearce (5)
Gisburn Road CP School

My First Acrostic - Poets From Lancashire

My Senses - Tasting

T oast is crunchy
A pples are tasty
S our are tomatoes
T omatoes are yummy
I ce cream is delicious
N ut biscuits are delicious
G rapes are yummy.

Kai Frankland (5)
Gisburn Road CP School

My Senses - Tasting

T oast crunching
A pples tasty
S ausages yummy
T omatoes sweet
I ce cream is cool
N uts are hard
G rapes are lovely.

Alisha Amer (5)
Gisburn Road CP School

My First Acrostic - Poets From Lancashire

Smell

S izzling sausages
M elting the frying pan
E ggs are smelly
L ovely flowers
L ovely sweets.

Anthony Collinge (6)
Gisburn Road CP School

Taste

T omatoes are sweet
A pples are juicy
S izzling sausages
T ea is tasty
E ggs are runny.

Tilly Falshaw (6)
Gisburn Road CP School

Smell

S izzling sausages.
M elons juicy.
E xtremely smelly compost bin.
L ovely lemons.
L ollies are sweet.

David Atkinson (6)
Gisburn Road CP School

Taste

Tea is sweet.

Apples and avocados are juicy.

Super sausages that are spicy.

Toast is scrummy.

Eggs are excellent.

Charley Berry (6)
Gisburn Road CP School

Taste

T oast is buttery
A pples are juicy
S ausages are yummy
T ea is hot
E ggs are runny.

Abid Zia & Kyle Rowan (6)
Gisburn Road CP School

Taste

Tasty toast.

Apples are red and juicy.

Sizzling sausages.

Tomatoes are red.

Eggs are runny.

Abigail Noon (5)
Gisburn Road CP School

Prehistoric Dinosaur

P rehistoric
A rmoured
R eptiles
A ngry
S cary giants
U nderground
A ttack
R oar dinosaur
O ld
L ong
O dd
P roud
H orn
U nusual
S trange creature.

Beth Fairclough (6)
Lathom Park CE Primary School

Dinosaurs

P terodactyls swoop from side to side
R eptiles run across the swamp
E ggs get eaten by other dinosaurs
H uge dinosaurs eat plants
I nteresting dinosaurs, like the T-rex
S wamp creatures eat plants in swamps
T riceratops has three horns on its head
O h the dinosaurs fly in the sky
R ocking dinosaurs rock and roll
I ncredible dinosaurs used to live on Earth
C lever dinosaurs are very clever.

Niamh Jefferson (5)
Lathom Park CE Primary School

My First Acrostic - Poets From Lancashire

Volcano

L ots of hot liquid,
A ll down the volcano.
V ery red and smoky,
A ll the dinosaurs dead in the mud.

James Sharrock (7)
Lathom Park CE Primary School

Dinosaur

T errible
R unning
I ncredible
C arnivore
E ggs
R eptiles
A mazing
T errifying
O dd
P layful
S wamp creature!

Ella Hutchinson (5)
Lathom Park CE Primary School

My First Acrostic - Poets From Lancashire

Carnivore

T all, terrible dinosaurs

R uns after others

E ats them up

eX tremely dangerous dinosaur!

Mia Aldred (6)
Lathom Park CE Primary School

All About Me

D iving

A dorable

N ightmare

I mpossible

E lastic

L oving.

Daniel Fogarty (4)
Lathom Park CE Primary School

All About Me

L ively
I mpish
L ovely
Y ummy.

Lily Sharrock (4)
Lathom Park CE Primary School

Year Two

Y ear Two is better than Year One
E very day in small assembly we have hymn books
A t the pantomime we are going to watch Mother Goose
R eading day is Wednesday

T he Great Fire of London is great
W e walk on Wednesday
O ur class has traffic lights.

James Kerr (6)
Littleborough CP School

My First Acrostic - Poets From Lancashire

Year Two

Y ou will really enjoy Year Two.
E xploding pictures was fun!
A t wet playtimes we either draw a picture or read a book.
R eading day is Tuesday.

T he resource area is amazing.
W e walk on Wednesday.
O ur science is materials.

Megan France (6)
Littleborough CP School

Year Two

Y ear Two is the best class in the world.
E xploding pictures are fantastic!
A t the library there are books and computers.
R eading day is on Wednesday.

T he resource area is fabulous.
W e are working on materials.
O ur topic is Mary Seacole.

Nathan Browne (6)
Littleborough CP School

My First Acrostic - Poets From Lancashire

Year Two

Year Two is the top infants.
Every day we go to assembly.
At the library we go on the computers.
Reading day is on Tuesday.

Topic work is about Mary Seacole.
We go to tuck shop at playtime.
Our class is the best!

Liam Simpson (6)
Littleborough CP School

Year Two

Y ear Two is good because you can make exploding pictures.

E veryone likes Mrs Mager.

A rchie's reading day is Wednesday.

R esource area is Friday.

T ry to stay on the green traffic lights.

W e visited the fire station.

O ur topic is Mary Seacole.

Archie Catlin (7)
Littleborough CP School

My First Acrostic - Poets From Lancashire

Year Two

Y ear Two is the best days I have!
E xploding pictures were cool!
A nd I like the people here.
R eading day is on Monday.

T he dining hall is big.
W alk on Wednesdays is good too.
O ur hall is for assembly.

Harry Ramsbottom (6)
Littleborough CP School

Year Two

Y ear Two visited the fire station.
E veryone goes to lunch.
A t school we do topic work.
R eading day is on Thursday.

T hursday we go to the library to change a book.
W e go to assembly every day.
O ur resource area is amazing.

Saffron Poskitt (6)
Littleborough CP School

My First Acrostic - Poets From Lancashire

Year Two

Y ear Two is the top class.
E very day we have playtime.
A t assembly we get to have hymn books.
R eading day is Thursday.

T he resource area is amazing.
W e do harder work.
O ur topic is Mary Seacole.

Freya Hollis (6)
Littleborough CP School

Year Two

Year Two teacher is nice, beautiful and the best.
Everyone goes to dinner at 12 o'clock.
At the library we change our books.
Reading day is on Thursday.

The resource area is amazing.
We have visited the fire station.
Our topic is about Mary Seacole.

Millie Harris (6)
Littleborough CP School

My First Acrostic - Poets From Lancashire

Year Two

Y ear Two is the top infants.
E very day we have assembly.
A t the library we go on the computer to do ICT.
R eading day is Tuesday.

T he resource area is on Friday.
W e are going to a pantomime called Mother Goose.
O ur science topic is materials.

Emily Dorrington (6)
Littleborough CP School

Year Two

Y ear Two is a really good year.
E very day we have milk and fruit.
A t the library we get to choose books.
R esource area is fantastic.

T here are traffic lights on the wall, if you go off you have not been good.
W e go to the computer suite on Thursday.
O ur topic is Mary Seacole.

Harvey Barker (7)
Littleborough CP School

My First Acrostic - Poets From Lancashire

Year Two

Y ear Two is fantastic.
E very day we have
A ssembly.
R eading day for me is Thursday.

T hursday is the day when we go to the resource area and paint,
make things, play in the water and sand.
W ednesday is walk to school day.
O n Tuesday we do gymnastics.

Matthew Williamson (6)
Littleborough CP School

Year Two

Y ear Two is utterly brilliant.

E very day we have playtimes.

A t our school we get to go in the resource area and paint, make things, play in the water and sand.

R eading partnership is when we read with Year Six.

T his term we went to visit the fire station.

W e have been learning about the Great Fire of London.

O n Tuesday we do gymnastics.

Adam Baker & Jacob Cockcroft (6)
Littleborough CP School

My First Acrostic - Poets From Lancashire

Year Two

Y ear Two is utterly brilliant.
E very day we have fruit and milk.
A t our school we get to go for walks.
R eading partnership is when we read with Year Six.

T his term we went to visit the fire station.
W e have been learning about the Great Fire of London.
O n Tuesday we do gymnastics.

Grace Shepherd
Littleborough CP School

Year Two

Year Two is very good!
Every day we have lunch
And on Wednesday we have walk to school.
Reading day for me is a Wednesday.

Tuesday is PE.
We have been to the fire station.
On Monday we do reading with Year Six.

Christopher Howarth
Littleborough CP School

My First Acrostic - Poets From Lancashire

Snake

S nakes like mice
N ight-time snakes curl up and sleep
A snake lives in a hole
K ills you if they are poisonous
E normous snakes can crush you.

Aadil Sarwar (6)
Manley Park Primary School

Tarantula

T arantulas can flick hairs.

A re poisonous.

R un fast.

A re hairy.

N asty and mean.

T arantulas are orange and black.

U gly.

L ong legs.

A re big.

Finn Moorhouse (6)
Manley Park Primary School

Hannah

H appy
A pples are my favourite fruit
N ice
N oisy
A bsolutely clever
H andy.

Hannah Iqbal (6)
Manley Park Primary School

Princess

P retty as a picture,
R eally good,
I am a princess,
N ever naughty,
C an be good and never naughty,
E at my favourite food,
S parkly dress,
S leeps a lot.

Imaan Talha (6)
Manley Park Primary School

My First Acrostic - Poets From Lancashire

Castle

C old, deep, damp and tall
A mazing castles
S words in the sky
T urrets are high
L ong and big
E normous.

Amanda MacKenzie (6)
Manley Park Primary School

Castles

C astles are a home for kings and queens,
A long flag,
S trong knights,
T all turrets,
L ovely queens,
E xcellent castles,
S trong castles.

Aqeel Ahmed (6)
Manley Park Primary School

My First Acrostic - Poets From Lancashire

Zebras

Z ebras are stripey
E ven people ride on them
B lack and white
R eally cute
A lways there.

Zaina Dar (6)
Manley Park Primary School

Dragon

D ragons are nasty,
R oar loudly,
A ngry,
G reedy,
O range and green,
N oisy and loud.

Mandeep Landa (7)
Manley Park Primary School

My First Acrostic - Poets From Lancashire

Isabella

I nterested in nature,
S hy at school,
A ble to talk at home,
B ig brain at work,
E veryone likes me,
L inked to animals,
L oves toys,
A mazing at colouring.

Isabella Rowles-Bennett (6)
Manley Park Primary School

Princess

P rincesses are so beautiful,
R eally good,
I nteresting,
N ice,
C ute,
E xcellent,
S mart,
S o pretty.

Arooj Shakoor (6)
Manley Park Primary School

Dragon

D ancing dragon,
R unning quite fast,
A really long-legged dragon,
G reat long tail,
O range and green,
N ot always scary.

Max Barrett (6)
Manley Park Primary School

Princess

P rincess,
R eally nice,
I n the top of the castle,
N ew long dresses,
C astles are where kings and queens live,
E very day in the castle,
S words are sharp,
S hields to protect them.

Abir Ahmed (6)
Manley Park Primary School

My First Acrostic - Poets From Lancashire

Flowers

F lowers are very pretty and have very pretty petals,
L ovely flowers in gardens and smell nice,
O range flowers in gardens,
W hen I smell flowers they smell nice,
E very day I smell my flowers,
R oses are very nice and smell nice,
S mell nice all the time.

Kiana Queeley (6)
Manley Park Primary School

Games

G ood fun for all.
A liens and monsters.
M onster truck.
E lephant game.
S trong slash.

Raj Abbas (7)
Manley Park Primary School

My First Acrostic - Poets From Lancashire

Pirate

P irates live on the old, dirty ship
I n the deep water lies the treasure
R ound and round goes the ship
A pirate with his parrot on his shoulder
T alk and talk all day
E ats pasta and bananas.

Cinderella Group (6)
Manley Park Primary School

Pirate

P arrot chatting happily
I n the ship lives a grumpy pirate
R ips the flags off the sails
A nd doesn't share the treasure
T ries to fight on his peg leg
E ats jellyfish and sharks.

Snow White Group (6)
Manley Park Primary School

My First Acrostic - Poets From Lancashire

Pirate

P irates have black patches
I n the water they go
R usty cutlass in their hands
A nd they want to find treasure
T hey follow a map to guide them
E veryone hates them!

Beanstalk Group (6)
Manley Park Primary School

Pirate

P irates eat fish fingers and chips
I slands in the middle of the sea
R ainbow up in the sky
A hungry shark waits at the plank
T reasure box full of gold
E nd of the Earth.

Gingerbread Man Group (6)
Manley Park Primary School

My First Acrostic - Poets From Lancashire

Pirate

P irates nervously walk the plank
I n the sea, waits the hungry crocodile
R ound and round sails the ship
A t the island they land
T hey dig for buried treasure
E arly in the morning.

Goldilocks Group (6)
Manley Park Primary School

Chhaya Patel

C arrying art stuff to make a
H at so it is colourful, I
H ate tidying my conservatory because it is
A lways messy because my
Y oung sister messes it up
A ll the time

P ainting and playing
A lways jumping in puddles
T rying my best
E ach day I work hard
L ove to play with my friends.

Chhaya Patel (6)
Markland Hill CP School

My First Acrostic - Poets From Lancashire

Madelaine Ramsden's Poem

M y favourite programme is X Factor.
A nimals are my favourite things.
D ads are my favourite parents.
E lephants are my favourite animal.
L ime is my favourite colour.
A rabbit likes carrots.
I love my family.
N abilah is my best friend.
E ggs are my favourite food.

Madelaine Ramsden (6)
Markland Hill CP School

Nabilah

N abilah is 6 years old.
A pples are my favourite fruit.
B ananas are my second favourite fruit.
I like the seaside.
L ovely lasagne is my favourite food.
A ugust is my best friend's month.
H ide and seek is my favourite game.

Nabilah Thagia (6)
Markland Hill CP School

My First Acrostic - Poets From Lancashire

Oliver's Poem

O liver is a kind boy
L oving and kind
I tidy up
V ery clever
E asy football game
R eally, Mrs Roberts is kind

L ike Mrs Pyke
E njoy school
A good learner
C reativity is my favourite thing
H olidays I like the very best.

Oliver Leach (6)
Markland Hill CP School

Isobel Jones' Poem

I love X Factor.
S ilver is my favourite colour.
O ctopus are my favourite animal.
B eans are my favourite food.
E lliot is my brother's name.
L illy is my best friend.

J ones is my last name.
O range is my worst colour.
N ever hit me because I will cry.
E mma is my cousin.
S almon is my worst food.

Isobel Alice Jones (6)
Markland Hill CP School

My First Acrostic - Poets From Lancashire

All About Me

G iggly and fun
R eally kind
A lways help Mum
C aring
E asy playing.

Grace Sohor (6)
Markland Hill CP School

Callum's Poem

C ool and loves Lois
A mazing kid
L ewis is amazing at maths
L ovely, lovely Lois
U pset
M ean friends

O ctopus boy
L oves Mum and Dad
D ad is cool
F ight tigers
I s clever
E njoys
L ooking
D oing things.

Callum Thomas Oldfield (6)
Markland Hill CP School

My First Acrostic - Poets From Lancashire

Ellis Richardson

E asy football games at school
L ikes Mrs Pike
L oves my brother
I saac is my brother
S am is my friend

R obert is in the juniors
I saac is sometimes annoying
C hristina is Isaac's favourite
H orses are big
A dam's in 3 Juniors
R oaring car
D addy is nice
S ometimes I go to the sweet shop
O n Sunday I go to football
N ot a very nice dog.

Ellis Richardson (6)
Markland Hill CP School

Benjamin

B all
E ating eggs
N ana
J umping
A mazing
M um
I s on the computer
N ever naughty.

Benjamin Hunt (5)
Markland Hill CP School

My First Acrostic - Poets From Lancashire

Sam

S uper writer
A mazing brother playing games
M ost of all Sam is good at writing.

Sam Davenport (5)
Markland Hill CP School

Lucas

L ikes helping
U nderwater swimming
C ake, fish and chips
A mazing
S izzling sausages.

Lucas Russell (5)
Markland Hill CP School

My First Acrostic - Poets From Lancashire

Hannah

H annah, eating red apples is good for me.
A nimals are very interesting.
N ice people are kind.
N ever be unkind.
A iesha lives near me.
H orses are great to ride.

Hannah Lay (5)
Markland Hill CP School

Luke

L aughing Luke
U mbrella
K ind Mummy
E xciting sweet shop.

Luke Anderson (5)
Markland Hill CP School

My First Acrostic - Poets From Lancashire

Ellie

E xcellent
L ikes reading
L ikes doing homework
I s a likeable girl
E xcellent at looking after people.

Ellie Rafferty (6)
Markland Hill CP School

My Favourite Things

S inging a concert makes people clap.

U nhappy people make me sad so I make them happy.

M aking a princess card is fun.

M ummy and Daddy give me big hugs.

E ating ham sandwiches, my favourite food.

R unning in a race I feel happy.

K icking a football is exciting.

A shton is my favourite brother.

Y ippee I am going to a party.

Summer Kay (5)
Markland Hill CP School

My First Acrostic - Poets From Lancashire

Jasmine

J umping and spinning at dancing.
A mazing at reading.
S wimming is fun.
M agic stuff is fun.
I ce skating is really fun.
N ice friends.
E ggs are nice.

Jasmine Lily Patel (6)
Markland Hill CP School

Sasha

S uper Sasha.
A mazing writing.
S pecial Sasha.
H appy friends.
A girl who rocks!

Sasha Palmer (6)
Markland Hill CP School

Kian

K ind Kian
I nteresting
A good boy
N ice Kian.

Kian Mistry (5)
Markland Hill CP School

Helena

H elena is natural.

E xciting when I ice skate.

L ovely girl.

E xcellent Helena.

N ever naughty.

A super friend.

Helena Lathwell-Watts (5)
Markland Hill CP School

My First Acrostic – Poets From Lancashire

Anuj

A mazing Anuj
N ever naughty
U nderstands lots of things
J umping, jolly boy.

Anuj Mishra (5)
Markland Hill CP School

James

J umping James B
A crobatics is fun
M ega runner
E xcellent person
S uper colouring person.

James Bewley (7)
Markland Hill CP School

My First Acrostic - Poets From Lancashire

My Special Friend

R ocking Rebecca is my friend.
E xcellent Rebecca and caring.
B eautiful as a butterfly.
E njoys playing peep behind the curtain.
C lever at writing.
C heerful as a bird.
A lways keeps a secret.

Cara Knowles (6)
St Joseph's RC Junior School, Leigh

My Special Friend

S uper Shannon is my friend.
H appy and smiling.
A lways helps me.
N ice and caring.
N early seven-years-old.
O wns a rabbit called Guiness.
N ever ever leaves me alone.

Ellie Taylor McDermott (6)
St Joseph's RC Junior School, Leigh

Amelia

A stonishing Amelia is my friend.
M akes me laugh.
E xcellent at singing.
L oving like a love heart.
I s as pretty as a flower.
A lways keeps secrets.

Shannon Roberts (6)
St Joseph's RC Junior School, Leigh

Hollie

H appy Hollie is my friend.
O wns two cats and two rabbits.
L ovely as a picture.
L ucky as treasure.
I mpossible to make her sad.
E xcellent at swimming.

Rebecca Clegg (6)
St Joseph's RC Junior School, Leigh

My First Acrostic - Poets From Lancashire

Daniel

Dazzling Daniel is my friend.
Always keeps a secret.
Never leaves me out.
Ideas in his mind.
Excellent at maths.
Listening Daniel.

James Clegg (6)
St Joseph's RC Junior School, Leigh

Aiden

A cting Aiden is my friend.
I deas in his mind.
D azzling like a star.
E xcellent at listening.
N ever lets me down.

Ben McDermott (6)
St Joseph's RC Junior School, Leigh

My First Acrostic - Poets From Lancashire

My Special Friend

H appy Hollie is my friend.
O wns two rats and three cats.
L oves to share.
L ikes to play peep behind the curtain.
I s pretty as a picture.
E xcellent at singing.

Amelia Tyrer (6)
St Joseph's RC Junior School, Leigh

Francesca

F abulous Francesca is my friend.
R uns like the wind.
A mazing at dancing.
N oisy as a monkey.
C ares for everyone.
E njoys swimming.
S ame smile every day.
C atches things and shows them to me.
A dmires my picture.

Hollie Hunter (7)
St Joseph's RC Junior School, Leigh

My First Acrostic - Poets From Lancashire

Amelia

A cting Amelia is my friend.
M akes me laugh.
E xcellent at writing.
L oving and caring.
I s as pretty as a flower.
A lways tells me jokes.

Cerys Knowles (6)
St Joseph's RC Junior School, Leigh

Ella

E xcellent Ella is my friend.
L oving and caring.
L aughing and joking.
A mazing and great.

Fiona Wilkinson (6)
St Joseph's RC Junior School, Leigh

My First Acrostic - Poets From Lancashire

Rebecca

R acing Rebecca is my friend.
E xcellent at swimming.
B ananas are her favourite fruit.
E njoys colouring.
C ake is her favourite food.
C heerful and it is hard to make her sad.
A lways cheerful at school.

Ellie Shepherd (6)
St Joseph's RC Junior School, Leigh

My Special Friend

L ovely Louis.

O wns a dog.

U nderstands me.

I s kind.

S hares secrets.

**Jack Bamford, Joshua Hedley, Louis Jackson Newn (6)
& Aiden Dungey (7)**
St Joseph's RC Junior School, Leigh

My First Acrostic - Poets From Lancashire

Shannon

S miling Shannon is my friend
H appy as a smile
A s brilliant as a jewel
N oisy as a tiger
N ever lets me down
O ld friends every time I sleep over
N ice as silver and gold.

Rebecca Wakefield (7)
St Joseph's RC Junior School, Leigh

Julia Woodworth

J ulia likes ice cream
U mbrella
L ikes playing with my sister
I like maths
A pples

W oodworth is my favourite second name
O ranges are my favourite fruit
O rang-utans are cool
D innertime
W oodworth is my favourite name
O reos are biscuits
R aisins are my favourite food
T rees are green
H urrah.

Julia Woodworth (5)
St Oswald's CE Primary School, Blackburn

My First Acrostic - Poets From Lancashire

Jack

J ack likes football
A nts
C ats
K arate.

Jack Crossley (5)
St Oswald's CE Primary School, Blackburn

Jacob

J elly
A pples
C ats
O ctopus
B ooks.

Jacob Crawford (5)
St Oswald's CE Primary School, Blackburn

My First Acrostic - Poets From Lancashire

James

J elly
A pples
M eat
E ating food
S ilence.

James Flynn (5)
St Oswald's CE Primary School, Blackburn

Sammy

S ammy is a good friend
A pples are my favourite
M um is nice to me
M ia is nice to me
Y ellow is my favourite colour.

Samantha Savage (5)
St Oswald's CE Primary School, Blackburn

My First Acrostic - Poets From Lancashire

Ellessa

E llie, Libby and Sam are my friends.
L ove my mum and my dad.
L ike my friends.
E llie is my friend.
S miley Ellessa.
S ome Bratz.
A ddison is my friend.

Ellessa Williamson (5)
St Oswald's CE Primary School, Blackburn

Mariyah

M ariyah likes ice cream

A pple

R abbits

I like playing with my sister

Y oghurts

A pples

H appy.

Mariyah Ahmed (5)
St Oswald's CE Primary School, Blackburn

My First Acrostic - Poets From Lancashire

Hafsah

H afsah likes ice cream
A pples are delicious
F lowers are my favourite
S unny Hafsah
A crostic poem
H appy person.

Hafsah Zubair (5)
St Oswald's CE Primary School, Blackburn

Brooklyn

B ubbly Brooklyn
R uns around
O rders pizza
O pens books
K icks footballs
L ikes ice cream
Y ellow tray
N ew in class.

Brooklyn Spiers (5)
St Oswald's CE Primary School, Blackburn

My First Acrostic - Poets From Lancashire

Addison

A ddison is fantastic.
D oes not like shepherd's pie.
D og.
I like ice cream.
S uper Ben 10.
O ctopus.
N othing frightens me.

Addison Cosgrove (5)
St Oswald's CE Primary School, Blackburn

Mia Dickinson

M ia is a good learner.
I like to play with my friends.
A lways works hard at the table.

D ogs are my favourite pet.
I like school.
C ats are my favourite animal.
K itchen helping Mum.
I like ice cream.
N ice and kind.
S ammy is my best friend.
O ranges.
N early six.

Mia Dickinson (5)
St Oswald's CE Primary School, Blackburn

My First Acrostic - Poets From Lancashire

Lucas

L ucas likes fish
U mbrella
C olouring
A pples to eat
S ilver.

Lucas Kennedy (5)
St Oswald's CE Primary School, Blackburn

Joshua

J oshua likes the zoo.

O n the trees.

S ammy.

H ome.

U mbrella.

A pples.

Joshua McDonald (5)
St Oswald's CE Primary School, Blackburn

My First Acrostic - Poets From Lancashire

Joseph

J oseph jumping
O ranges
S weets
E ats apples
P laying
H appy.

Joseph Campbell (5)
St Oswald's CE Primary School, Blackburn

Domenico

D ark hair.
O utstanding in PE.
M usic I like to listen to.
E ducation is what I get at school.
N ewspapers I like to read.
I ntend to do my best.
C ranes I would like to ride.
O melette is my favourite food.

Domenico Nelson (6)
St Oswald's CE Primary School, Blackburn

My First Acrostic - Poets From Lancashire

Cameron

C ars are fast and I love speed.
A rmy is cool, they keep us safe.
M y mum buys me biscuits.
E lephants and aeroplanes I love.
R unning is my favourite sport.
O ctopus are amazing, they squirt ink!
N ature is nice!

Cameron Carruthers (6)
St Oswald's CE Primary School, Blackburn

Joshua

J uggler I wish I could be
O ctopus I wish I could see
S oaring I am at night
H appy when I ride my bike
U nbelievable I wish I could ride
A mazing I am.

Joshua Parrington (6)
St Oswald's CE Primary School, Blackburn

My First Acrostic - Poets From Lancashire

Faye

F riendly and happy.
A lways do my best.
Y ellow is my favourite colour.
E xcellent at colouring.

Faye Filbin (6)
St Oswald's CE Primary School, Blackburn

Corey

C reamy smoothie and soft on the outside
O h I went camping at the weekend
R ed steamy face when I get angry at home
E xcited to go camping with my uncle and my dad
Y es I want to go shopping at Morrisons

W hoa I didn't know we were going to Pontin's
A ha I know we are going to the Redcap.
L arry and friend, let's go to the park
S o I want to play with you
H ey will you be my friend?

Corey Walsh (6)
St Oswald's CE Primary School, Blackburn

My First Acrostic - Poets From Lancashire

Scott

S chool teaches me to learn
C amels are what I like to see
O range is my favourite colour
T uesday is my favourite day
T hank you for animals.

Scott Duffy (6)
St Oswald's CE Primary School, Blackburn

Fatima

Fireworks I love to watch.

Ace at literacy.

Tennis I am good at.

Ice cream I like it.

March is the month of my birthday.

Always kind and helpful.

Fatima Lodge (6)
St Oswald's CE Primary School, Blackburn

My First Acrostic - Poets From Lancashire

Joe

J ubilant and jolly day.
O utstanding at making friends.
E specially good at making friends.

Joe Banks (6)
St Oswald's CE Primary School, Blackburn

Lewis

L ovely brown eyes.
E ngineer is what I would like to be when I leave school.
W izard at doing maths.
I nquisitive I always am.
S wimming is my favourite hobby.

Lewis Heyn (6)
St Oswald's CE Primary School, Blackburn

My First Acrostic - Poets From Lancashire

Brandon

B atman is my favourite superhero.
R acing is my best hobby.
A valanches are cool because I like watching the snow fall down.
N ervous when starting school.
D oughnuts I think are great stuff.
O vals are really nice because they are curvy.
N oisy I am because I love playing.

Brandon Parkinson (6)
St Oswald's CE Primary School, Blackburn

Louise

L ovely I am, I am . . . I adore myself.
O utstanding I am . . . everybody says.
U K is where I live . . . I like where I live.
I ce cubes I love in my lemonade.
S abre-tooth tigers I love even though they are extinct.
E lephants are my favourite animals. Elephants have long trunks. Elephants never forget anything and neither do I!

Louise Cullen (6)
St Oswald's CE Primary School, Blackburn

My First Acrostic - Poets From Lancashire

Abbie

Always a smile on my face.
Bridesmaid is what I would like to be.
Bananas are my favourite fruit.
Improvement is what I want to achieve.
Entertain all my friends at school.

Abbie Bausor (6)
St Oswald's CE Primary School, Blackburn

Bailey

B eautiful, like the teachers.
A lways getting on with my work.
I ce cream I love.
L isten to teachers all the time.
E njoy my work, especially maths.
Y oghurt is my favourite healthy food. *Yum, yum, yum, yum!*

Bailey Madden (6)
St Oswald's CE Primary School, Blackburn

My First Acrostic - Poets From Lancashire

Friends

F riends are excellent, they are nice to me.
R iding skateboards together.
I don't like my friends fighting because they make me flabbergasted.
E veryone loves me because I love them.
N athanial is my friend because I play with him.
D ogs play together.
S o never play with a bully because they will be nasty to you.

Alex Burrows (6)
Sacred Heart Catholic Primary School

Friends

F riends make me happy and friends make me feel fantastic

R ichard makes me happy

I like my friends and my friends like me

E veryone likes me and I like them

N o playing with big bullies

D on't hit people because it isn't nice

S mashing friends, I like my friends.

Ebony Pennington (7)
Sacred Heart Catholic Primary School

My First Acrostic - Poets From Lancashire

Friends

F riends are smashing.
R iding bikes.
I like friends to play with me.
E very day friends play with me.
N ever play with a bully.
D o not play with a big bully.
S ome people play with me because I am lonely.

Nathan James Daly (6)
Sacred Heart Catholic Primary School

Friends

F riends are good to me
R iding on bicycles together
I like friends because they play with me
E verybody stays with pure people
N asty bullies are bad to me
D avis is good to me
S mashing people are my friends.

Sam Birch (6)
Sacred Heart Catholic Primary School

My First Acrostic - Poets From Lancashire

Friends

F riends play football.
R iding our big bikes together.
I like my friends.
E verybody likes Sam because he is funny.
N o bully can play with me.
D on't play with a stinky bully.
S am is my best friend.

Davis Lythgoe (6)
Sacred Heart Catholic Primary School

Friends

F riends are good to me
R eally good friends come to my house
I like my animals climbing trees
E veryone likes me because I am cool
N aughty friends are ratbags
D on't mess with my friends
S mashing friends.

Oliver Whittle (7)
Sacred Heart Catholic Primary School

My First Acrostic - Poets From Lancashire

Friends

F riends are kind to me
R iding big scooters
I like my friends
E verybody likes my comics
N o one likes an evil bully
D oughnuts make me and my friends happy
S uper friends make me happy.

Matthew Best (6)
Sacred Heart Catholic Primary School

Friends

F riends make me happy
R iding bikes together
I like my friend Ebony
E bony is kind
N ever likes stinky bullies
D o play with lonely people
S ad friends, I help them.

Anna Zwolinska (6)
Sacred Heart Catholic Primary School

My First Acrostic - Poets From Lancashire

Friends

F riends are fabulous
R iding with friends
I care about my friends
E ach friend is God's gift to you
N o friends are bad to you
D on't bully people
S uper friends are happy people.

Lennon Pennington (6)
Sacred Heart Catholic Primary School

Friends

F riends play good games with me
R iding big BMXs in the water
I like making friends together
E verybody is my friend
N obody likes being with a bully
D o play with lonely people
S mashing friends.

Adam Pilkington (6)
Sacred Heart Catholic Primary School

My First Acrostic - Poets From Lancashire

Friends

F riends are cool.
R iding on bikes through the forest.
I like my friends because they are brilliant.
E veryone likes me.
N ever play with a bully.
D o play with sad people.
S am is my best friend!

Joshua Cain (6)
Sacred Heart Catholic Primary School

Friends

F riends play together
R iding big BMXs in the water
I play with my friends
E verybody is my friend
N o one is my enemy
D o play with lonely people
S mashing friends.

Aidan Dickinson (6)
Sacred Heart Catholic Primary School

My First Acrostic - Poets From Lancashire

Friends

F riends make me happy
R ichard is my name
I love my friends because they are mine
E xtra friends make me happy, they think I am a scream
N obody plays with bullies
D o play with friends
S mashing friends make me flabbergasted.

Richard Nelson (6)
Sacred Heart Catholic Primary School

Me!

P hoebe loves playing!
H ates cheese.
O ranges
E ats them all day!
B eing friends with
E veryone.

Phoebe Banks (6)
Turton & Edgworth Primary School

My First Acrostic - Poets From Lancashire

Erin

E rin saw an elephant.
R ead a book.
I love ice cream.
N ever saw a zebra.

Erin Louise Gardiner (5)
Turton & Edgworth Primary School

Isaac At The Zoo

I went to the zoo
S aw a big tiger
A nd I saw a big lion
A nd I saw a monkey
C ame home.

Isaac Earnshaw (5)
Turton & Edgworth Primary School

My First Acrostic - Poets From Lancashire

Friends

F unny friends
R unning
I ce-skating
E ach day
N ow we are
D ancing and
S inging.

Rebecca Sheldon (5)
Turton & Edgworth Primary School

Friends Forever

F reinds
R ead a book
I n the quiet corner
E verybody wants to read
N ew books and old books
D aisy likes to read
S uper reading!

Daisy Grace Mather (5)
Turton & Edgworth Primary School

I Love Trains

J oshua is happy
O n trains
S team engines
H urry
U p and down
A long the track.

Joshua Aubrey (6)
Turton & Edgworth Primary School

Up And Down

L ibby is a good girl
I n school
B ut at home she is bad
B ouncing on the bed
Y o-yo up and down.

Libby Faye Roberts (5)
Turton & Edgworth Primary School

My First Acrostic - Poets From Lancashire

James Likes Jam

J ames likes jam
A nd honey
M y favourite thing is to play
E lephants are now on the door
S tepping in.

James White (6)
Turton & Edgworth Primary School

Aneurin

A neurin has some friends
N ay has some friends
E very day they play football
U nder the sky
R un fast
I love jam
N ext day.

Aneurin Walsh (5)
Turton & Edgworth Primary School

My First Acrostic - Poets From Lancashire

James Fox

J ames is a superstar
A nd smart
M y friends Jacob and Cameron
E very day we play
S tar Wars and have

F un
O n the
X -box.

James Joseph Fox (5)
Turton & Edgworth Primary School

Harvest

H arvest leaves fall off the branches and turn brown.
A utumn leaves blow around in the gusty wind.
R ain falls on the ground and it makes a massive puddle.
V egetables grow from the ground and when they are ready you pick them.
E veryone starts to collect all the leaves and crops.
S quirrels gather their nuts when they fall on the ground.
T ractors and farmers collect in the crops.

Libby Bradbury (7)
Watersheddings Primary School

My First Acrostic - Poets From Lancashire

Harvest

H arvest leaves turn orange and red.
A utumn leaves fall off the trees.
R ain falls on the ground, makes a puddle.
V egetables stop growing and are picked.
E verybody gathers crops.
S quirrels eat nuts that are on the ground.
T rees blow in the wind, makes the leaves blow down.

Hana Karim (6)
Watersheddings Primary School

Harvest

H arvest leaves start to fall.
A utumn leaves blow.
R oses are growing.
V egetables are gathered.
E verybody gathered the crops.
S quirrels get the nuts.
T hey pull up to get the crops.

Joseph Sargent (6)
Watersheddings Primary School

My First Acrostic - Poets From Lancashire

Harvest

H arvest leaves turn orange and brown.
A nimals fall asleep.
R ain dries off the trees onto my head.
V egetables are carried from fields.
E veryone gets vegetables.
S quirrels collect nuts.
T ractors pull up the potatoes to eat.

Nicole Sweeney (6)
Watersheddings Primary School

Harvest

H arvest leaves turn brown, red and orange.
A utumn leaves fall off the trees.
R ain falls off the leaves and makes puddles.
V egetables are picked out of the ground.
E veryone is eating hot food.
S quirrels are collecting nuts.
T ractors are getting the potatoes.

Sarah-Jane McDonald (6)
Watersheddings Primary School

My First Acrostic - Poets From Lancashire

Harvest

H arvest leaves turn yellow, orange, brown and red.
A utumn leaves fall off the trees.
R ain sometimes drops and makes big puddles.
V egetables get picked.
E veryone gathers leaves.
S quirrels get the nuts.
T ractors and farmers get the crops.

Lara Bardsley (6)
Watersheddings Primary School

Harvest

H arvest vegetables, carrots, potatoes and onions
A farmer digs up the food and vegetables
R ain falls in puddles and makes bigger puddles
V egetables get collected and put into harvest bags
E veryone collects their vegetables
S quirrels gather their nuts ready for winter
T ractors can be seen in fields and on the farm.

Paiden Ball (7)
Watersheddings Primary School

My First Acrostic - Poets From Lancashire

Young Writers Information

We hope you have enjoyed reading this book - and that you will continue to enjoy it in the coming years.

If you like reading and writing poetry drop us a line, or give us a call, and we'll send you a free information pack.

Alternatively if you would like to order further copies of this book or any of our other titles, then please give us a call or log onto our website at www.youngwriters.co.uk.

Young Writers Information
Remus House
Coltsfoot Drive
Peterborough
PE2 9JX
(01733) 890066